RUSSIAN PUNCHNEEDLE EMBROIDERY

With Instructions and 32 Transfer Patterns

GAIL BIRD

Dover Publications, Inc.
New York

I wish to acknowledge the following people for their many contributions in design, information and support: Jean Cook, Marinda Brown, Mary Manocchio, Linda Nakashima, Barbara Michelsen and Gwen Wagner Amos. A special thanks to my wonderful supportive husband, Dick, and my helpful, loving, and tolerant children, Melody, Randy, and Kristy. A special thanks to Rita Weiss, who encouraged and supported this endeavor.

Published in Canada by General Publishing Company, Ltd., 30 Lesmill Road. Don Mills, Toronto, Ontario.
Published in the United Kingdom by Constable and Company, Ltd., 10 Orange Street, London WC2H 7EG.

Russian Punchneedle Embroidery is a new work, first published by Dover Publications, Inc., in 1981.

International Standard Book Number: 0-486-24146-7
Library of Congress Catalog Card Number: 81-66593

Manufactured in the United States of America
Dover Publications, Inc.
31 East 2nd Street
Mineola N.Y. 11501

INTRODUCTION

Punchneedle embroidery is the art of working one basic stitch with special needles to create a raised ornamental design on woven fabric. A variety of beautiful effects, details and textures can be achieved by using this stitch with different size needles, threads and fabrics. There are several forms of punchneedle embroidery, but the most versatile is the Russian folk style. Although the history of Russian punchneedle is not fully documented, it is thought that a group of people called the "Russian Old Believers" created this style of embroidery using fine needles and threads. Other cultures had practiced punchneedle, but primarily as a decorative art; the Russians used this technique to embellish their costumes and icon panels.

Today punchneedle embroidery is popular as a hobby, a craft and an art form. It can be used to decorate fashion accessories such as purses, necklaces, combs, belts, pins, earrings, scarves, shawls, and aprons; it can add a designer touch to shirts, blouses, skirts and dresses as well. Punchneedle embroidery can embellish home furnishings and accessories such as pillows, wall hangings, mirror or picture frames, fabric boxes, sachets, tablecloths and napkins too! Many hobbyists use punchneedle to create miniature rugs, pillows and furnishings for doll houses. There is no limit to the items you can embroider, and as you become more familiar with the technique, you will probably develop your own specialty, perhaps one that has never been done before.

In order to do Russian punchneedle embroidery, a hollow needle threaded with floss is punched from the wrong side of a woven piece of fabric, leaving a loop of yarn on the right side. When this simple procedure is repeated in a precise, neat manner, the result is a surface of loops, referred to as the pile. These loops create the design; they can be short and close to the surface, or they can be long—long enough, in fact, to shear and sculpt! This book is a complete guide to the Russian style of punchneedle embroidery, and contains descriptions of the equipment needed, detailed instructions for stitching, and transfer patterns for punchneedle.

The designs in this book were created especially for Russian punchneedle embroidery by artists skilled in the craft.

HOW THE PUNCHNEEDLE WORKS

The punchneedle is a long hollow tool with an eye (or hole) at its sharp, pointed end. The thread passes through the tube and then the eye. As the needle punches through the fabric, a loop of thread is left on the underside. One of the design features of punchneedle embroidery is the variation that can be achieved with different loop sizes. The size of the loop is determined by the distance between the eye and the stopper, a small, generally adjustable gauge such as a plastic sleeve that fits snugly on the needle. The length of the gauge controls the depth the needle can pierce the fabric. Check your needle instructions for ways to vary the loop size.

There are several brands of punchneedles on the market. Most are gauged to the common cotton 6-strand embroidery floss and are made in graduating sizes to hold various amounts of floss: A small size needle holds 1 strand, medium size holds 2 or 3 strands, and the large size holds 4, 5 or 6 strands. It is not possible to use a single strand in any but the small size needle; larger needles leave a hole in the fabric too big to hold a one-strand loop.

The smallest needle is the one used to create the traditional Russian punchneedle embroidery; the larger embroidery needles are a recent adaptation. As a general rule, the smaller the needle, the shorter the loop and the more intricate and detailed the design; the larger the needle, the longer the loop and the less detailed the design.

EQUIPMENT AND MATERIALS FOR PUNCHNEEDLE

You will need a threader, embroidery thread, fabric, an embroidery hoop, scissors, and a pattern—any one of the iron-on transfer designs in this book will be perfect.

NEEDLE CHART

NEEDLE SIZE	#1	#3	#6
FABRIC WEAVE	tight weave	tight to medium weave	medium to loose weave
FABRIC WEIGHT	lightweight	light to medium weight	heavy weight
THREAD	1 strand of 6-strand embroidery floss sewing machine thread silk thread	2–3 strands of floss #8 pearl cotton buttonhole twist thread	4–6 strands of floss #5 pearl cotton
*SIZE OF STITCH	$\frac{1}{32}$"	$\frac{1}{16}$"	$\frac{1}{8}$"
**SIZE OF LOOPS (minimum)	$\frac{1}{8}$"	$\frac{3}{8}$"	$\frac{1}{2}$"
DESIGN	small areas highly detailed	medium-size areas some detail	large areas little detail
DISTANCE BETWEEN ROWS	Always leave some fabric showing on the back or stitching side. The amount of space between the rows depends on needle size, size of stitch taken, and fabric weave and weight.		

*Stitch size is usually the same measurement as the diameter of the hollow metal tube.
**Loop size is one-half the measurement from the eye of the needle to the gauge.

Needle Diagram

THREADING THE PUNCHNEEDLE

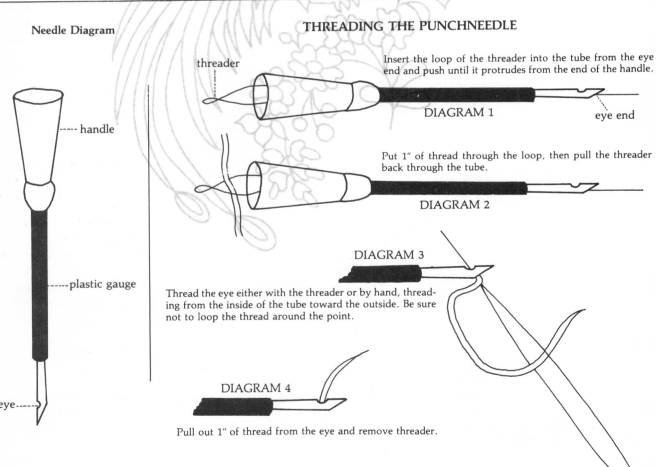

threader

Insert the loop of the threader into the tube from the eye end and push until it protrudes from the end of the handle.

DIAGRAM 1

eye end

Put 1" of thread through the loop, then pull the threader back through the tube.

DIAGRAM 2

DIAGRAM 3

Thread the eye either with the threader or by hand, threading from the inside of the tube toward the outside. Be sure not to loop the thread around the point.

DIAGRAM 4

Pull out 1" of thread from the eye and remove threader.

---- handle

----- plastic gauge

eye -----

Instructions continue following transfer patterns.

PLATE 1

PLATE 1

PLATE 2

TEST PATTERN

PLATE 2

PLATE 3

PLATE 3

PLATE 4

PLATE 4

PLATE 5

PLATE 5

PLATE 6

TEST PATTERN

PLATE 6

TEST PATTERN

PLATE 7

PLATE 7

PLATE 8

TEST PATTERN

PLATE 8

TEST PATTERN

PLATE 9

TEST PATTERN

PLATE 9

PLATE 10

TEST PATTERN

PLATE 10

PLATE 11

PLATE 11

PLATE 12

TEST PATTERN

PLATE 12

PLATE 13

PLATE 13

TEST PATTERN

PLATE 14

TEST PATTERN

PLATE 15

PLATE 15

PLATE 16

PLATE 16

TEST PATTERN

PLATE 17

PLATE 17

PLATE 18

PLATE 18

PLATE 19

PLATE 19

PLATE 20

PLATE 20

PLATE 21

PLATE 21

PLATE 22

PLATE 22

PLATE 23

PLATE 23

PLATE 24

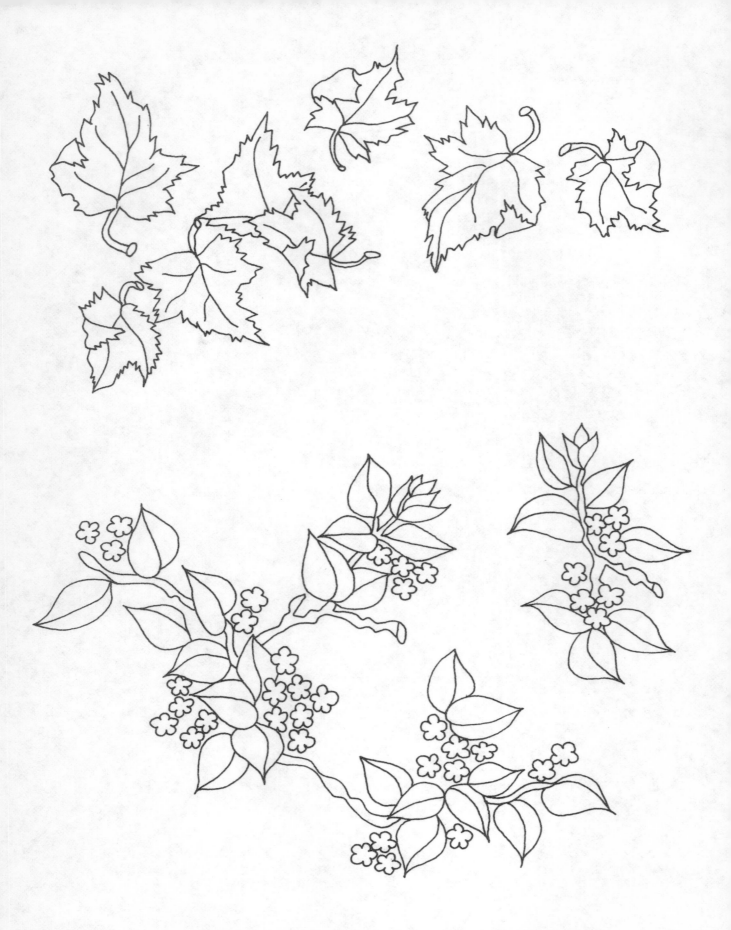

PLATE 24

The Threader: The threader is a long, thin, folded wire with a loop at the fold. It is a delicate implement, but it is an important component, so treat it with care. Most punchneedles are packaged with a threader, because in addition to threading the eye of the needle, you must also thread the tube; see the diagrams for Threading the Punchneedle.

The usual technique for threading a punchneedle is as follows: Insert the loop of the threader into the tube from the eye end and push until it protrudes from the end of the handle. Put 1" of thread through the loop, then pull the threader back through the tube. Finally, thread the eye either with the threader or by hand, *threading from the inside of the tube toward the outside.* Be sure not to loop the thread around the point. After a little practice, this step becomes fast and easy; read the manufacturer's directions for your needle for any special instructions in threading.

Threads: Threads are available in such a wide variety of colors that an almost limitless palette is available for "painting" in this artform. The most commonly used thread is cotton embroidery floss, but many others can be used, including Pearl cottons and synthetic threads. Generally, these threads are spun and therefore have a twist which is important for the punchneedle technique. The needle carries the thread through the fabric, but as it is withdrawn, the thread is left as a loop which untwists so the loop "balloons" larger than the hole produced by the needle. Because of the untwisting process, thread should not be reused.

Check the quality of the thread you buy; if it is not spun evenly it may have thick sections which will plug your needle—or thin ones which can break.

Constant re-threading can slow down punchneedle work, so to keep it moving, cut your thread in 3' long pieces. If the thread comes on a spool, use it directly from the spool without cutting.

For small needles, floss must be separated into strands. For a 1-strand needle, tightly pinch the 6 strands of floss about ½" from one end; using the other hand, pick out a single strand and pull it straight up, keeping the pinch tight and allowing the thread to bunch up under your fingers. Continue to pull out one strand at a time. To separate two or more strands, fold the floss in half and tightly pinch a small loop of floss in the middle. Then, as above, pull the number of threads desired straight up from the tight pinch.

It is fun to experiment with different kinds of threads, using different colors mixed in a needle, or mixing different kinds of thread in a design. For an elegant effect, we used metallic threads in some of the designs in this book.

Fabrics: Choose any kind of woven fabric made from natural fibers or blends. Wash all fabrics before you begin to work to shrink them and remove sizing which tends to make the needle drag or stick. The most important factor in choosing a fabric is the weave. When using a small needle, the fabric must be tightly woven. Tightness of weave is indicated by the number of threads per inch; the higher the number, the tighter the weave. Sheeting and broadcloth are good examples of tightly-woven fabrics. If you plan to use a larger needle, choose a fabric with a medium weave; refer to the needle chart and test your fabric with a few practice stitches. For the designs in this book we used a tightly woven, lightweight polyester/cotton blend.

Hoops: A hoop that will stretch the fabric board-tight and keep it that way is ideal. Use a plastic hoop that has a lip on the inner ring. A good-quality wooden hoop can be used if the inner ring is wrapped with yarn or twill tape. Hoops are available in many sizes, but a 5" or 6" one is the most desirable; smaller hoops require more changes in position on large designs; larger hoops are hard to handle, and may not keep the fabric tight enough.

Don't be afraid to place the hoop on finished punchneedle work. Crushed pile can be restored by holding a steam iron above it and coaxing the loops back in position with your fingers. It is best to remove the hoop from the fabric when interrupting work for a lengthy period; this avoids soiling your work or the fabric at the lip edge.

Scissors: There is no knotting in this technique. Loose threads are cut on the back side, flush with the surface of the fabric; loose threads or "tag" ends on the front side are cut to the level of the pile. Sharp, flat 4" embroidery scissors are best because they can lay flush with the surface when cutting. If the scissors are dull, the cut will not be clean and the thread can catch and be pulled out. If this happens, rake the fabric weave back together with your fingernail, and repunch that area.

Patterns: The patterns in this book were designed specifically for 1-strand and 3-strand needles. Typical color schemes for punchneedle embroidery are shown in the finished designs on the covers.

Remember to iron the transfer onto the *wrong* side of the fabric. If you wish to combine punchneedle with other embroidery techniques, hold the fabric up to a window and trace the design lines onto the right side. This will be necessary for the fine running stitch lines explained in Special Techniques.

DIRECTIONS FOR STITCHING

Transfer the pattern to the fabric following the directions opposite. Stretch the fabric, transfer side up, board-tight in the hoop; the fabric is tight enough when a penny dropped on it will bounce off, and you can "ping" it with your fingers. Thread your needle, allowing 1" of thread to extend from the eye. Now, begin stitching, following the How to Stitch diagrams.

Punch the needle straight down until firmly stopped by the gauge—the first stitch should make a popping sound. Raise the needle out of the fabric, but not off the surface. Scratch the needle across the fabric, one needle width, to begin the next stitch. Orient the needle so the eye "looks" at the stitch just made. Repeat the process, and continue stitching.

Work the outline of the design first, then fill the spaces, beginning with small areas such as eyes or flower centers. Embroider by following the design lines, or by stitching in rows according to the fabric weave. You should not be able to see fabric between the loops on the right side; however, do not allow rows to touch each other on the wrong side. Leave some space between rows to avoid puckering the fabric when it is removed from the hoop.

To stop stitching, let the thread run out through the needle, or hold onto the last stitch and gently slide the needle away. Cut all threads as close to the surface as possible on the back side, then trim away all "tags" on the front side. Washing the finished piece will not only freshen it, but will tighten the fabric weave so the loops will be held more securely in place. To further guarantee that the loops won't pull out, you can apply a thin coating of fabric glue over the stitches on the wrong side.

CORRECTING PROBLEMS

There may be times when your punchneedle loops do not form perfectly or hold securely in the fabric. If so, go over the following list of trouble spots to see where your problem originates.
* the fabric is too loose in the hoop
* the stitches are too far apart
* the weave of the fabric is not correct for the needle size
* the needle is threaded improperly
* there is tension on the thread (check for slubs, kinks or knots in the thread; make sure the thread is the correct thickness for the needle)
* the punch is not perpendicular to the fabric
* the thread is not trailing out of the eye in a direct line with the previous stitch

HOW TO STITCH

DIAGRAM 1

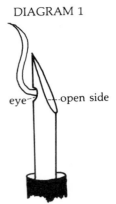

eye — open side

Examine the needle to familiarize yourself with the open side and the eye.

DIAGRAM 2

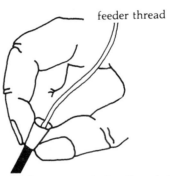

feeder thread

Hold the needle by grasping the handle and allowing the feeder to flow freely over your hand. Never obstruct the feeder thread.

DIAGRAM 3

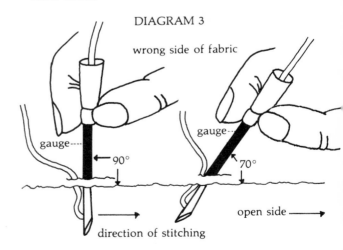

wrong side of fabric

gauge — 90°

gauge — 70°

direction of stitching

open side →

Decide upon the direction in which you will stitch, then orient the needle with the open side facing that direction. Punch the needle straight down (90° angle) or at a slight angle (no less than 70°) until firmly stopped by the gauge.

DIAGRAM 4

wrong side of fabric

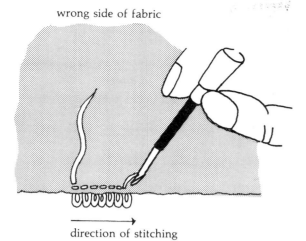

direction of stitching

Raise the needle out of the fabric, but not off the surface. Scratch the needle across the fabric, one needle width, to begin the next stitch. Orient the needle so the eye "looks" at the stitch just made.

DIAGRAM 5

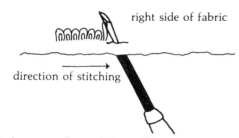

right side of fabric

direction of stitching

If stitches are small enough they will form a continuous line of loops on the right side of the fabric.

DIAGRAM 6

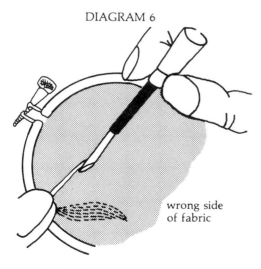

wrong side of fabric

To stop stitching, hold onto the last stitch with your thumb and gently slide the needle away.

SPECIAL EFFECTS FOR PUNCHNEEDLE EMBROIDERY

After you have mastered the basic techniques of punchneedle embroidery, you may want to try some of these special effects:

Velvet: For a richly-colored velvet texture, hold your scissors in three different ways:

Shearing: Holding the scissors parallel to the surface, cut long loops like a lawnmower.

Clipping: Holding the point of the scissors perpendicular to the pile, cut open each individual loop; this is used when the pile is not long enough to shear.

Sculpting: Shape masses of long loops by holding scissors at an angle and snipping around the sides toward the center until a rounded shape is formed.

Uneven Pile: Work loops with no consistent pile depth to create an uneven texture.

Reverse Punch: For a flat, running stitch effect such as on flower stems, vines, strings, etc., trace the design onto the right side, then punch from the front to the back.

Beading: For a unique treatment of eyes, flower centers and other small areas, leave space in the desired area, then sew on colored seed beads with a beading needle to fill in the space.

When you practice punchneedle embroidery, see that your lighting is good, and that you are seated in a comfortable position—you'll be surprised at how quickly you will achieve precision and rhythm, and how fast your work will go.

If you need equipment information or if you would like to share the fun with other enthusiasts throughout the country in a newsletter, send a stamped, self-addressed envelope to:

Gail Bird
PUNCHLINE
P.O. Box 837
Patchogue, New York 11772

DIRECTIONS FOR USING TRANSFER PATTERNS

Transferring the designs to your fabric is a fairly simple procedure. Here are directions for using these transfer patterns.

Prepare the Fabric: If the fabric is washable, preshrink and remove the sizing by laundering first. Iron carefully to remove all wrinkles. If the fabric ravels, whip-stitch the edges by hand or zigzag-stitch the edges by machine. Since transfers are made with very high temperatures which might melt synthetic fabrics, use a fabric with some natural fiber content such as cotton or linen. If you are unsure of the fibers in your fabric, test the ironability of the fabric first.

Prepare the Ironing Board: To prevent the motif from transferring to your ironing board, place an old sheet or other smooth fabric over the ironing board cover. To obtain a stronger impression of the pattern —especially after the transfer has been used, or on darker fabrics—place a piece of aluminum foil on your board before pressing.

Make a Test Transfer: Before beginning any project, it is a good idea to test your iron, the fabric and the evenness of your hand pressure. Cut out one of the motifs marked "Test Pattern" and follow the directions below for making a transfer. If the ink transferred well, you can proceed; if not, adjust either the heat or the length of time.

Transfer the Patterns:

1. Use a *dry* iron on the wool setting.

2. Place the fabric on the ironing board, *wrong* side up.

3. Cut out the desired motifs, allowing a margin around the edges of the design. Pin the design to the wrong side of the fabric with the printed side down. Place the pins through the margins to hold the transfer in place on the fabric. Protect the iron by placing a sheet of tissue paper between the transfer and the iron.

4. Place the heated iron on the transfer and hold down for about 5 seconds. Apply a firm, downward even pressure to all parts of the design, being especially careful to get the outer edges, such as the tips of leaves and flowers. Do not move the iron back and forth across the fabric as this will cause the transfer pattern to blur. After the transfer has been used once, add 2–3 seconds for each additional transfer.

5. Carefully remove one pin and lift one side of the transfer paper to see whether the complete design is indicated on the fabric. If not, replace the pin and repeat the process, concentrating on the area that did not transfer. Do not remove all the pins until you are sure the design has been successfully transferred.

Once the pattern has been unpinned it is almost impossible to register it to the fabric again.

6. When you are satisfied that the transferring has been completed, unpin the transfer paper and peel it off. You will want to save the transfer paper to use for additional repeats (you can usually get four or more transfers from each pattern) or to use as a check on the design. If the design is not clear enough, you can refer to the transfer sheet and reinforce vague areas on the fabric with a waterproof felt pen. Make sure that the ink is completely waterproof because just the moisture from a steam iron can cause the ink to run and ruin your embroidery.

Special Instructions for Use on Dark Fabrics: If you wish to use these patterns on dark fabric on which transfer ink will not show up, or if you need additional repeats of the same transfer, put a piece of tracing paper over the uninked side of the transfer and trace the design. Discard the original transfer paper and pin the tracing in place on the fabric. Slip a piece of dressmaker's carbon, color-side down, between the fabric and the tracing; do not pin the carbon. With a hard, even pressure, trace a few lines with a tracing wheel, stylus or similar tool. Raise one corner of the tracing and the carbon to check the impression. If the results are too faint, apply more pressure; if too heavy, less pressure. After adjusting the impression, trace the entire design and then remove the carbon and carefully remove one pin to see whether the design is intact on the fabric *before removing the pattern.*

IMPORTANT

Since these transfer patterns are made to be used more than once, the ink will not readily wash out of the fabric. This is of no concern to those using the patterns for punchneedle embroidery. However, if these designs are used for other embroidery techniques, be sure to cover all design lines with stitching.

Dover Publications assumes no responsibility for any damage to fabrics caused by the transfer inks in this book.
